Fixing the Dollar Now

Why US Money Lost Its Integrity and How We Can Restore It

Judy Shelton
SENIOR FELLOW
CO-DIRECTOR OF SOUND MONEY PROJECT

Fixing The Dollar Now:
Why US Money Lost Its Integrity and How We Can Restore It
by Judy Shelton

Copyright © November 2011
Atlas Economic Research Foundation

Copyedited by Susannah Hickling
Cover Design & Layout by Cassy Loseke

For information and other requests, please write:
Atlas Economic Research Foundation
1201 L Street NW, Second Floor
Washington, DC 20005
AtlasNetwork.org

ISBN: 978-0-9639638-1-9

Printed in the United States of America

This publication was made possible with generous funding from the Searle Freedom Trust.

Contents

Introduction

The idea of 'fixing' the dollar can have various meanings. In the international sense, it can mean fixing the exchange rate of the dollar to other currencies. Or it can mean fixing the value of the dollar to some kind of universal measure of monetary value, such as gold. But it could also mean fixing the dollar because it is broken and no longer provides a meaningful way to measure productive growth in the real economy.

This last meaning is the one that will receive our primary attention in this study because it goes to the heart of what the United States needs to do to reclaim its virtue as well as renew its economy.

For some, the word 'virtue' may seem out of place in a treatise on money, finance, and economic issues. We usually reserve such terms for subjects involving moral behavior. But what is money if it does not accurately and reliably serve as a measure of value – so that people can make decisions with confidence based on prices in a free market economy? What is money if it cannot be trusted as a store of value?

The whole purpose of money is to provide a dependable measure – to function as the recognized unit of account – so that individuals are able to carry out financial and economic transactions efficiently. When the money is broken, it fails to perform this fundamental role in society; it feeds a certain distrust of markets in general. People may feel they have accumulated a certain amount of wealth through hard work and planning, only to see it all disappear as the stock market goes into meltdown. Of course, no one expects guaranteed outcomes when savings are put at risk; it's the nature of capitalism to fund productive investments with the financial 'seed corn' that has been put aside by people as foregone consumption. When you have confidence that your savings will be used in a way that will lead to greater resources in the future, when you believe that the merits of an investment have been accurately evaluated based on projections of future returns, you are willing to sacrifice today for a better tomorrow.

But what if it all turns out to be a con game?

What if the money that you were relying on to convey accurate signals about the value of investments were being manipulated by its issuer to help achieve a different set of objectives? Prime examples would be making it easier for the government to sell its debt instruments or encouraging people to purchase homes they could not afford. These goals may not seem nefarious *per se*; they might even be defended in the name of serving the public good.

While a free people can decide what government priorities should be – indeed, it is their duty as citizens – the disturbances to free market interactions when money has been distorted are more damaging than the presumed benefits would justify. Does it make sense to allow the issuer of US money, the Federal Reserve, to purchase the debt issued by the US government through a process that expands the number of dollars in the system? Is it really socially beneficial to lure people into taking on mortgages by manipulating interest rates and creating government-subsidized lending programs?

Can it possibly be worth compromising the integrity of the monetary unit of account for the US population as a whole – not to mention the impact of dollar distortion in the global marketplace – just to enable our government to influence credit allocations in pursuit of its own objectives for engineering the economy? If money serves such a vital function in maintaining the viability of democratic capitalism by furnishing an accurate tool of measurement and meaningful store of value, should it be so easily yielded up to government as a policy instrument?

The main argument in this treatise is that private sector determination of the money supply results in more effective utilization of financial and economic resources than government-controlled money unrestricted by any kind of automatic discipline – in other words, subject only to 'discretionary' monetary authority. In terms of political philosophy, it is akin to placing more faith in the wisdom of the free marketplace as expressed in the aggregate decisions of countless individuals than relying on the omniscient judgment of a handful of government-appointed officials. It is not to say that the Chairman of the Federal Reserve or other members of the board of governors, who comprise the policy-making committee of the Fed, have less-than-stellar qualifications or less-than-noble intent. It is rather to suggest that *any* such committee seeking to direct financial flows of investment capital through the American economy – immense in its complexity, diversity and dynamism – has already overestimated its own capabilities.

What's more, it has exceeded the intended monetary authority granted to government by our nation's Founders. In the Constitution, the power of Congress to coin money and regulate its value is conveyed in the same context – indeed, in the very same sentence (Article I, Section 8) – as the power to fix the standard of weights and measures.

Our money was always meant to serve as a standard.

That is the conclusion drawn in this study after researching the early debates among our Founders regarding the money powers that might be safely granted to Congress. It was not an authority easily rendered; they well understood the temptation for government to abuse its money powers by conferring legal tender status on its own promissory notes. This was to be prevented by defining the US dollar in specific weights of precious metals. As Thomas Jefferson wrote in 1784: 'If we determine that a Dollar shall be our Unit, we must then say with precision what a Dollar is.[1]

And far from dismissing this early assertion of dollar integrity as a parochial vestige from a former age, this study will reveal that it was consistent with a sophisticated appreciation for international commerce. It showed America's eagerness to take advantage of opportunities for foreign trade by participating in an integrated monetary system. Then as now, the domestic benefits of having a dependable money unit dovetailed with the potential to reap economic rewards through engagement with the rest of the world.

Today, the overwhelming power of the Federal Reserve to distort the value of our currency is a far cry from having a dollar fixed to gold and silver. We will examine why this quasi-government agency was permitted to become a financial behemoth. This will be accomplished by tracing the slow erosion of limitations on the money powers granted to Congress. By understanding the specific turning points in history leading to our current situation, where the government's borrowing needs are commingled with

3

its monetary authority, we become better positioned to challenge the status quo. We gain greater credibility in arguing that our founding principles make it incumbent on the provider of US money, the issuer, to guarantee the integrity of the dollar.

Again, we speak in moral terms when referring to money. This is because the trustworthiness of America's unit of account is a profoundly moral issue. It impacts the value of wages, taxes, savings and investments for hundreds of millions of individuals who make countless decisions based on daily prices. If we can't trust the money, we can hardly believe in the virtues of free enterprise itself.

The ultimate purpose of this publication is to put forward new solutions for restoring the integrity of the US dollar. We need to erase the mistakes that have put the Federal Reserve at the center of defining the dollar's value; we need to end the practice of having our 'elastic' currency serve as the default mechanism for government fiscal irresponsibility. Even among well-intentioned monetary officials, a budgeting stalemate begets situational morality. We need to instill automatic discipline through gold convertibility. At the same time, however, we have to recognize that the transition process needs to be eminently workable at the domestic level as well as globally viable.

America's economic leadership in the world will ring hollow until we restore our own credibility – and quite literally, our creditworthiness – by reining in the Federal Reserve's unrestrained authority to compromise our nation's currency. This needs to be accomplished as part of a broader agenda aimed at limiting the government's overall role in the economy. That agenda should encompass fiscal transformation through a balanced budget, a streamlined pro-growth tax code, a new emphasis on the wealth-generating capacity of individuals under free market conditions and the pursuit of greater prosperity through expanded trade relations.

In short, our goal should be to foster individual freedom and economic opportunity.

Fixing the dollar is where we begin.

Part One

The Fall From Grace

Like most instances of moral decline, the loss of virtue associated with our nation's currency took place slowly, over a long period of time. The steps delinking the US dollar from its original purpose as an unchanging standard of value occurred incrementally at distinct points in our history.

In every case, there was a pragmatic reason for doing so; that is, practical people could justify making some adjustment to the constitutional authority granted to Congress in order to deal with an exigency. It was prompted by financial concerns for the nation in some cases; on other occasions, it was motivated by political considerations. Always it resulted in a weakening of the intrinsically valuable definition of the dollar. And thus, it further impinged on the private property rights of the individual who relied on the dollar to maintain its constancy as a standard of value.

Why US money lost its integrity is a story of capitulation in the name of principled compromise and forward thinking. Effectively, it is the triumph of rationalization over conscience – because it is clear the Founders believed that a depreciating currency was anathema to the cause of liberty.

In this section, we will first review the original ideas presented by American statesmen concerned about the potential for monetary abuse by government authorities. Next we will proceed to examine the pressures that came to bear on this earlier resolve to maintain sound money. Finally, we will study how this slow drift brought us to our current situation, where the value of a dollar is a matter of government decree, not intrinsic worth.

BEGINNING PRINCIPLES: "CERTAIN VALUE"

Modern observers of monetary policy might be forgiven for thinking their forebears were unable to comprehend the complexities of foreign currencies being used alongside domestic ones. One might be tempted to believe that they blindly accepted 'bills of credit' – in other words, government-issued banknotes representing government debt -- as legal tender. And it's easy to think that our contemporary world of foreign exchange markets and quantitative easing by the Federal Reserve is wholly different, that it somehow matters whether depreciation of the money unit took place back then as opposed to now.

But let's read the concerns of Roger Sherman more than two centuries ago:

> I think it is a principle that must be granted that no government has the right to impose on its subjects any foreign currency to be received in payments as money which is not of intrinsic value; unless such government will assume and undertake to secure and make good to the possessor of such currency the full value which they oblige him to receive it for. Because in so doing they would oblige men to part with their estates for that which is worth nothing in itself and which they don't know will ever procure him any thing.
>
> Rhode Island Bills of Credit have been so far from being of certain value and securing to the possessor the value that they were first stated at, that they have depreciated almost four seventh parts in nine years last past, as appears by their own Acts of Assembly. For in the year 1743, it appears by the face of the Bills then emitted that twenty-seven shillings Old-Tenor was equal to one ounce of silver. And by an Act of their General Assembly passed in March last, they stated fifty-four shilling Old-Tenor Bills equal to one ounce of silver, which sunk their value one half. By another Act in June last, (viz 1751) they stated sixty-four shillings in their Old-Tenor Bills equal to one ounce of silver.[2]

Clearly, this Connecticut patriot – Sherman was the only person to sign all four great state papers of the US: the Continental Association, the Declaration of Independence, the Articles of Confederation and the Constitution – well understood the injustice dealt to any citizen who is required by government to accept money having less than *certain value* as legitimate payment. Sherman exhibited a keen awareness that the depreciation of the money unit is nothing more than insidious thievery. He notes that the bills of credit issued by the government of neighboring Rhode Island (when colonies were independent) had lost more than half their value over a nine-year period. Readily acknowledging the advantages of having a common medium of exchange 'of intrinsic and unchanging value', he writes:

> But if what is used as a medium of exchange is fluctuating in its value, it is no better than unjust weights and measures, both which are condemned by the laws of God and man, and therefore the longest and most universal custom could never make the use of such a medium either lawful or reasonable.[3]

This aversion to paper money was shared by George Washington, who saw its tendency toward depreciation as a threat to the cohesion of the fledgling independent nation comprised of individual states. In a letter to Jefferson on August 1, 1786, the man who would shortly become the first President of the United States observed that some of the states were 'falling into very foolish and wicked plans of emitting paper money'.[4] For Washington, the problems unleashed by paper currency were related to the inevitable abuse of the monetary privilege; when governments can obtain credit by issuing promissory notes, which are then used as the medium of exchange for conducting transactions, it is the honest producers who are hurt by currency debasement. As he explained to Thomas Stone, a member of the Maryland Senate, in a letter written on February 16, 1787:

> ...consequently depreciation keeps pace with the quantity of the emission, and articles, for which it is exchanged, rise in a greater ratio than the sinking value of the money. Wherein, then, is the farmer, the planter, the artisan benefited?[5]

It's hard to imagine a more succinct definition of inflation and its deleterious impact on commerce.

James Madison, primary author of the Constitution, was equally concerned. 'Paper money is unjust', he wrote in notes prepared for an address before the Virginia Assembly in November 1786. Citing the unfairness of changing weights and measures, he argued that paper currency encouraged 'extravagance' and fostered 'an unfavorable balance of trade'. Ultimately, it had the effect of 'destroying that confidence between man and man, by which resources of one may be commanded by another'. In short, Madison denounced non-interest-bearing credit notes issued by government - paper money - as being 'unconstitutional' because a depreciating currency 'affects the rights of property as much as taking away equal value in land'.[6]

There can be no question that our nation's Founders deliberately sought to ensure that the new government they were about to install at the federal level would never be able to indulge in the same monetary fraud that had brought ruin and cynicism to individual states. No longer would self-serving state governments be entitled to issue credit notes for their own use and have the power to force citizens to accept these instruments as lawful currency; no longer would paper money subject to depreciation function as the medium of exchange among citizens across the various states.

To attribute monetary value to the credit notes issued by government at the federal level would be to compound the mistakes already made by the states and refuse to learn any lesson from them. It would also undermine the cohesion necessary to form a viable new nation answerable to its own citizens. Alexander Hamilton, who would serve as the first United States Secretary of the Treasury, affirmed in his own evaluation of what needed to be done to forge a successful federal government that monetary abuse was inconsistent with the aspirations and principles of the people. As he set forth explicitly in his resolutions for a new Constitution of the United States of America:

> To emit an unfunded paper as the sign of value ought not to continue a formal part of the constitution, nor ever hereafter to be employed; being, in its nature, pregnant with abuses, and liable to be made the engine of imposition and fraud; holding out temptations equally pernicious to the integrity of government and to the morals of the people.[7]

Hamilton's reference to the 'integrity of government and to the morals of the people' clearly indicates that even among those who favored a strong central government with autonomous powers, it would be anathema to the cause of self-government to permit the issuance of credit

8

notes to serve as legal tender.

By the time Jefferson had completed his own study on how to establish an official money unit for the United States and how to proceed with coining this new medium of exchange to serve as a common currency to be used across state lines, the parameters were clear. In his *Notes on Coinage*, Jefferson stressed the importance of having a fixed unit of money that would 1) be convenient for people to use in their daily life, 2) have easily calculated proportions among its various divisions and 3) comport with the value of the most familiar and trusted coins already in use.

It is instructive that Jefferson put so much emphasis on the need for people to be able to trust their money – this new coinage that would help unite citizens in the creation of a budding nation. Money would, for the first time in history, be based on a decimal approach in order to simplify the arithmetic for conducting transactions. Commerce should not be burdened with complex arithmetic and awkward measuring units, Jefferson reasoned. Nor should money be subject to varying rates of exchange between the different states; a fluctuating money unit would stymie, rather than encourage, economic growth through expanding trade relations.

Jefferson was firmly convinced that American money should provide a dependable and unchanging standard of value. Indeed, he hoped it might one day establish a worldwide standard. In one of his first acts as Secretary of State, Jefferson submitted a 'Plan for Establishing Uniformity in the Coinage, Weights, and Measures of the United States' to the House of Representatives calling for such straightforward and universal standards. And it is evident from comments made by Washington in his earliest directives as President to the newly-formed Congress that Jefferson greatly influenced him on this matter. In 1790 Washington stated:

> Uniformity in the currency, weights, and measures of the United States is an object of great importance, and will, I am persuaded, be duly attended to.[8]

Nearly two years later he remained unwavering in this belief:

> A uniformity of weights and measures is among the important objects submitted to you by the Constitution, and, if it can be

derived from a standard at once invariable and universal, it must be no less honorable to the public council than conducive to the public convenience.[9]

Reflecting this desire for openness, honesty, simplicity and uniformity in establishing the official standards for America – including the monetary standard – the ideas and principles of the Founders were brought to fruition by the Coinage Act, which was passed by the US Congress on April 2, 1792.

Officially entitled 'An Act Establishing a Mint, and Regulating the Coins of the United States', the legislation laid out the precise specifications for American coins, which were to serve as the nation's money of account. In accordance with the pioneering decimal approach, it was determined that US money would be expressed in dollars (the unit of account), dimes (tenth of a dollar), cents (hundredth of a dollar) and even milles (thousandth of a dollar). The dollar itself, or unit, was to be equal in value to the Spanish-milled dollar currently in wide use across America; it was to contain 371.25 grains of pure silver. A coin equal to ten dollars (or units) – an 'eagle' – was to be struck out of 247.50 grains of pure gold. In addition, there would be minted half-eagles (123.75 grains of pure gold) and quarter-eagles (61.875 grains of pure gold) and also half-dollars (185.625 grains of pure silver) and quarter-dollars (92.8125 grains of pure silver). Dimes and half-dimes were to be struck in silver in exact proportional relationship to the silver content of dollars, while cents and half-cents were to be minted in specific weights of copper.

It's enlightening to examine this money law in such detail because it makes it very clear that the Founders had a rigid interpretation of the limited money powers granted to government by the Constitution. 'Regulating' the money of account for the United States meant specifying the precise definition of this vital measure in gold, silver and copper. It also meant that America's money unit would accord with the Spanish dollar, or 'pieces of eight' coin, already in broad use among the states. The gold and silver coins were to have the inscription 'Liberty' and the year of coinage on one side, with the figure of an eagle represented on the reverse side along with the inscription 'United States of America'. Notably, although it had initially been suggested that all coins carry a portrait of the President on the obverse side, the final draft of the legislation stipulated the simple inscription 'Liberty' instead.

So the money unit of account for the nation, implemented with great care and following great debate by our Founders, was to be the dollar as defined in terms of precise weights of gold or silver. The limited monetary authority granted to Congress by the Constitution is expressed in Article I, Section 8: 'To coin Money, regulate the Value thereof, and of foreign Coin, and fix the Standard of Weights and Measures'. There can be no doubt that US money was to provide a standard of value as dependable and constant as the official weights and measures it would likewise adopt. In combination with the proscription in Article I, Section 10 against states being allowed to 'make anything but gold and silver coin a tender in payment of debts', the new common currency of the United States was born.

It is worth quoting the following section of the Coinage Act of 1792 to fully appreciate that 'regulating' the value of US money, as far as the Founders were concerned, meant that authorities at the mint were expected to be scrupulous in ensuring that the money standard, as defined, was conscientiously maintained:

> *And be it further enacted*, that if any of the gold or silver coins which shall be struck or coined at the said mint shall be debased or made worse as to the proportion of the fine gold or fine silver therein contained, or shall be of less weight or value than the same ought to be pursuant to the directions of this act, through the default or with the connivance of any of the officers or persons who shall be employed at the said mint, for the purpose of profit or gain, or otherwise with a fraudulent intent, and if any of the said officers or persons shall embezzle any of the metals which shall at any time be committed to their charge for the purpose of being coined, or any of the coins which shall be struck or coined at the said mint, every such officer or person who shall commit any or either of the said offenses, shall be deemed guilty of felony, and shall suffer death.[10]

RATIONALIZED DRIFTING

How did such an unambiguous commitment to honest money from our early history as a sovereign nation seemingly become an anachronism? Why did we drift away from beginning principles regarding the moral aspects of trustworthy money - the notion that a fluctuating medium of exchange was 'no better than unjust weights and measures', in the words of Sherman? What made us ignore Washington's instruction that the value of the monetary standard should be 'invariable and universal' or that currency debasement with fraudulent intent was a felonious act warranting the harshest punishment?

The fact is some of the reasons for muddling the clear directives adopted by the Founders and veering off the monetary course laid out by the Coinage Act of 1792 were related to minor changes in the ratio of gold to silver. Other departures occurred in conjunction with wartime expenditures and a few key deviations were aimed at circumventing the convertibility of US money into specie – in other words, gold or silver.

And then there was the establishment of the Federal Reserve System in 1913, created to provide an 'elastic' currency.

Since the monetary history of the United States spans more than two centuries, this overview will be necessarily brief. What emerge, however, are the main themes involving changes in the monetary integrity of US currency. It is important to understand when adjustments were made for economic reasons, for political reasons, to finance wartime expenditures on a temporary basis – or to more permanently empower government through centralized banking.

We begin with economic issues arising from the decision to define the dollar in terms of both gold and silver, which necessarily meant that the value of the two precious metals used as US money was fixed at 15 to 1; indeed, the Coinage Act of 1792 explicitly sets this proportional relationship as a matter of law.[11] Moreover, the US mint was obligated to assay and rapidly coin into US money any amount of gold or silver bullion brought to it by any person – and to do so free of charge.[12]

When either silver or gold increased in value due to market demand (because both metals have nonmonetary uses, for jewelry or industrial purposes) people would rationally decide to mint the less valuable metal as money while utilizing their holdings in the other metal at its higher commodity value. Both gold and silver could legally serve as lawful tender, so why not use the cheaper metal?

The value of gold began to increase very slightly relative to silver in the years following the adoption of the Coinage Act. As a result, people brought silver to the mint to be coined – which could then be exchanged at the fixed rate for the more valuable gold. Over the next few decades, the United States was effectively on a silver standard; cheap money drove out dear money, fulfilling the economic logic known as 'Gresham's Law'. Keep in mind that the ratio between gold and silver was 15.625 to 1 on world markets by 1834, hardly a huge shift. Still, a decision by Congress that year to change the official ratio to 16 to 1 reflected political and economic pressures to encourage the circulation of both gold and silver coinage, while at the same time discouraging the use of paper currency issued by private banks.

Changing the ratio, however, triggered the opposite trend and gold began to replace silver as the preferred metal for monetary purposes. The dollar was still defined as 371.25 grains of pure silver but the gold metal content for the ten-dollar eagle coin was reduced to 232.20 grains of pure gold from its earlier 247.50 grains. So now it was more logical for people to use gold as money – a condition that persisted until the 1890s, when a 16 to 1 ratio would once again favor silver. (Students of US history will recall the heated presidential campaign of 1896, during which William Jennings Bryan proclaimed: 'You shall not press down upon the brow of labor this crown of thorns, you shall not crucify mankind upon a cross of gold.')

But two very significant events took place during this extended period, both of which impacted the integrity of US money.

First, of course, came the devastating Civil War from 1861 to 1865. Seeking to raise vast new funds to pay for the fighting on behalf of the Union, Congress authorized the issuance of fiat money – the infamous 'greenbacks' – not redeemable in either gold or silver. Greenbacks circulated in parallel with gold as people continued to conduct some transactions in gold, others in the newly issued paper money. Banks cooperated by offering their clients separate deposit accounts in gold and greenbacks. It wasn't long before the non-interest bearing US notes fell substantially in value relative to the established national money, to less than 50 cents on the dollar within two years.

What made the issuance of greenbacks particularly controversial was the designation of legal tender status – each carried the inscription 'This Note is a Legal Tender' – which meant the paper currency had to be accepted as payment by a creditor despite the fact that it was not backed by gold. 'The bill before us is a war measure,' argued Elbridge G. Spaulding, a New York congressman who supported the Legal Tender Act of 1862. 'These are extraordinary times, and extraordinary measures must be resorted to in order to save our government, and preserve our nationality.'[13]

13

But many disagreed, citing the limited money powers granted to government by the Constitution. Specifically, they highlighted the fact that the Founders had empowered Congress only 'to coin money' and had not authorized it to compel people to accept its own credit notes as lawful tender.

It is telling to cite the personal example of Salmon P. Chase, who served as Secretary of the Treasury when greenbacks were first issued and who had helped formulate the enabling legislation. President Lincoln subsequently appointed him Chief Justice of the Supreme Court. In 1870, Chase joined the majority of the Court in ruling that the Legal Tender Act of 1862 was a violation of the Constitution. (The following year, the decision was reversed when two new justices to the Court decided that the Legal Tender Acts were constitutional after all and that debtors could repay debts in greenbacks rather than gold or silver specie as specified by contract.)

The other major event to influence the virtue of the dollar as a monetary standard was far more subtle, though it resonated with those who had grown suspicious of government's commitment to preserving the value of the nation's money unit.

Anxious to return to a specie standard following the greenback episode, Congress passed the Coinage Act of 1873, which authorized the minting of various gold and silver coins – but omitted the silver dollar coin comprised of 371.25 grains of pure silver that had served as the historical US money unit. Even though a specie standard based on gold was successfully resumed in 1879, the switch from a bimetallic standard to a monometallic standard meant that silver would no longer be minted as money at the former 16 to 1 ratio. This increased demand for gold as money and caused a general deflation in prices. (The more scarce the money, the more it is worth, hence prices are lowered in exchange for the money.)

Since farmers are generally debtors, this group of citizens felt particularly squeezed by having to repay loans in more expensive gold money. The 'Crime of 1873' slogan that animated the 1896 presidential campaign was a rallying cry on their behalf to allow prices to rise in accordance with more plentiful silver supplies.

William McKinley, who favored a gold standard, prevailed over his opponent. Ironically, he went on to preside over an economic boom in which prices rose as new gold discoveries substantially increased the money supply and helped fuel an expansion. Meanwhile, the triumph of the gold standard aligned the US monetary system with the gold-standard currencies of the United Kingdom, France and Germany. Moreover, it reaffirmed the 1834 definition of a gold-backed dollar in terms of its metal content – 23.22 grains of pure gold – which implied a dollar price for gold of $20.67.[14]

This $20.67 rate of dollar convertibility into gold would reign until January 31, 1934, when President Franklin Roosevelt issued an executive proclamation devaluing the gold dollar from $20.67 to $35 per troy ounce of gold. The day before, redemption of paper currency for gold was terminated; minting and circulation of gold coin was stopped, and citizens were required to surrender all gold coin and certificates. These drastic steps were the culmination of a series of emergency measures begun a year earlier under Roosevelt in response to the ongoing financial crisis following the October 1929 stock market crash. Interestingly, Roosevelt had hoped to rehabilitate silver as a monetary metal and had promised to convene an international monetary conference for that purpose immediately after his inauguration. But even though the government proceeded to issue silver certificates exchangeable for silver coin, depressed silver prices ensured that the paper money was not converted.

In short, the suspension of gold convertibility in tandem with a presidential decree forbidding the 'hoarding' of gold meant that American citizens were effectively deprived of any kind of specie-linked dollar to serve as their monetary standard. The US government would continue to define the dollar in terms of gold – but only for purposes of conducting official settlement transactions with the central banks of other countries.

Central banks had begun to gain in importance as facilitators in providing capital for growing industrialized nations. Concerns over periodic banking panics and problems caused by seasonal variation in the need for currency to carry out transactions had created demands for more flexibility in supplying money. Long before the problems associated with the Great Depression of the 1930s, the Federal Reserve Act of 1913 authorized the creation of a central banking system that included twelve regional banks owned by participating commercial banks. The Fed would make temporary funds available to banks to satisfy unanticipated customer demands for cash, and it would create a new form of money –

Federal Reserve notes – which could be expanded or contracted to provide more cash as needed.

It is important to keep in mind that the establishment of the Federal Reserve did not change the fact that the United States remained on the gold standard in 1913. The dollar was still defined as a specific weight of gold and Federal Reserve notes were redeemable in lawful money. Indeed, even when most of Europe was forced off the gold standard under the financial pressures of World War I from 1914 to 1918, the United States maintained gold convertibility for American citizens while briefly regulating its export.

But the combination of severe economic downturn and the exercise of vast new emergency powers by government some two decades later would largely put an end to the Founders' concept of defining the US money unit as a precise weight of gold or silver. Paper notes and checks were fast replacing coins – and redemption had become a moot point in any case.

Still, there was a sense that a stable monetary foundation was needed if the world was to recover from the collapse in trade and economic output during the Depression years leading up to the outbreak of World War II in Europe in 1939. Dollar convertibility for individual citizens may have been largely abandoned, but governments understood the importance of being able to define their own currencies in terms of a universal measure; if not gold, then what?

GLOBAL DOLLAR ANCHOR

Even as war was raging overseas and the US had just been attacked at Pearl Harbor on December 7, 1941, the US Treasury Secretary was already considering how best to establish a postwar international monetary system. Henry Morganthau was concerned that the Allied forces in Europe had little motivation to prevail over the Axis powers if they could not look forward to a more ordered and prosperous world than the one they had known in the previous decade. He asked his deputy, Harry Dexter White, to consider options for coordinated monetary arrangements among the United States and its Allies.

White soon prepared a draft memo proposing the establishment of two different institutions, a special multilateral bank to supply cheap loans to Allied countries, and an international monetary fund to stabilize foreign exchange rates and encourage the flow of productive capital. By April 1942, White had laid out a detailed plan that would eventually result in the creation of the International Bank for Reconstruction and Development (now known as the World Bank) and the International Monetary Fund (IMF).

White was particularly committed to the importance of stable exchange rates as the key to raising prospects for world economic performance:

> The advantages of obtaining stable exchange rates are patent. The maintenance of stable exchange rates means the elimination of exchange risk in international economic and financial transactions. The cost of conducting foreign trade is thereby reduced, and capital flows much more easily to the country where it yields the greatest return because both short-term and long-term investments are greatly hampered by the probability of loss from exchange depreciation. As the expectation of continued stability in foreign exchange rates is strengthened there is also more chance of avoiding the disrupting effects of flights of capital and of inflation.[15]

The concept was transformed into an international monetary arrangement among participating nations following the adoption of the Articles of Agreement worked out in July 1944 at a conference held in Bretton Woods, New Hampshire. What came to be called the 'Bretton Woods system' was a fixed-exchange rate regime that started operations in December 1945 with a membership of 39 countries. On joining, each nation was required to submit payment to the IMF in accordance with its assessed 'quota' based on relative economic importance and level of international transactions. Voting power and borrowing rights were also determined by this quota amount. Each nation had to pay 25 per cent of its quota in gold and the remaining 75 per cent in its own national currency.

The essence of the Bretton Woods international monetary system was its reliance on the US dollar to serve as the key reserve currency which anchored the whole arrangement. Other nations tied their own currencies to the dollar at fixed rates, which meant the former 1930s practice of using currency depreciation to procure a temporary trade advantage (by making exports less expensive when priced in other currencies) was no longer possible. During the Depression years, nations had successively devalued against gold and finally abandoned the gold standard. But the new Bretton Woods approach to stabilizing exchange rates was meant to establish a solid base on which to build trade and financial relationships around the world so that economies could recover and flourish in the postwar era.

However, the system depended crucially on the dollar to retain its integrity as a valid monetary standard. Because the dollar was technically convertible into gold at the rate declared by Roosevelt in 1934 – $35 per troy ounce of gold – the ultimate anchor for the system was the same metal that had disciplined money issuance for centuries. But it was a far cry from the earlier gold standard, which permitted individual citizens to redeem paper money for specie on demand. And it was wholly different from the embodiment of value in actual coins. Whereas the Founders had defined the dollar as a precise weight of gold or silver and conscientiously ensured that minted coins served as a reliable unit of account, medium of exchange and store of value – there being no distinction between the value of US money and its intrinsic worth – the dollar under Bretton Woods was American currency that could be redeemed in gold only by foreign governments and central banks.

Still, while monetary discipline was not automatic, the link to gold sufficed to act as a brake against runaway inflation. Political considerations prevented foreign governments from exercising their right to exchange accumulated US dollars for gold at the fixed rate of $35. In other words, as the United States became Europe's protector from the threat posed by the Soviet Union in the 1950s and 1960s, it seemed ungrateful for Western Allies to demand absolute fiscal discipline from America. Despite complaints by French leader Charles de Gaulle that the United States enjoyed an exorbitant privilege as issuer of the world's reserve currency, there was no alternative to the dollar. It was the only major currency tied directly to gold – even though the link was growing increasingly tenuous.

As the pressures of massive social spending during the late 1960s under President Lyndon Johnson combined with the costs of fighting a war in Vietnam, the monetary consequences of budgetary excess grew more severe. Because other currencies were fixed to the dollar, the issuance of more dollars by the Federal Reserve to cover the spending gap in Washington meant that other nations had to increase the issuance of their own currencies. Every time Americans imported goods from abroad and paid for them with new dollars, the central banks of those nations had to provide their own citizens with the equivalent amount of domestic currency at the fixed rate. Effectively, the United States could export its own inflation around the world with little concern that its trade partners would challenge the authority of the key currency nation.

However, the deteriorating monetary situation was becoming untenable by the beginning of the 1970s. Rising inflation and unemployment were now impacting the domestic American economy. Other nations too were growing bolder about asserting the right to convert debased dollars into gold at the promised $35 rate. Foreign governments knew that to insist on redemption would be to force the collapse of the Bretton Woods system. But they also felt the US government should face up to its global responsibilities, and take steps to resolve the international monetary crisis and initiate meaningful reform.

On August 15, 1971, President Nixon met with Treasury Secretary John Connally, Federal Reserve Chairman Arthur Burns, economist Herbert Stein and Paul Volcker (who was Treasury Under Secretary for Monetary Affairs at the time) at Camp David to confront the impending problem of foreign gold redemption and to devise a strategy for heading off an embarrassing financial catastrophe. Later that Sunday evening, the strategy was announced: the United States would no longer permit foreign governments or central banks to redeem US dollars in gold.

In the aftermath of the final delinking of US money from gold, the dollar gyrated as oil prices quadrupled and the world experienced its deepest recession since the 1930s. Along with it came a new phenomenon called 'stagflation', in which rising prices co-existed with high unemployment in industrial countries. Sensing that untethered currencies would ignite trade tensions and ultimately hurt economic growth prospects, European governments began planning in earnest to develop their own common currency as an alternative. Meanwhile, the value of the dollar would deteriorate markedly in terms of its domestic purchasing power, declining more than 82 per cent during the 40-year period of floating rates from 1971 to the present.[16]

Decades after the collapse of the Bretton Woods system, Paul Volcker, who was later charged with managing an out-of-control US money supply as Federal Reserve Chairman from 1979 to 1987, reflected on the outcome:

Increases of 50 per cent and declines of 25 per cent in the value of the dollar or any important currency over a relatively brief span of time raise fundamental questions about the functioning of the exchange rate system. What can an exchange rate really mean, in terms of everything a textbook teaches about rational economic decision making, when it changes by 30 per cent or more in the space of twelve months only to reverse itself? What kind of signals does that send about where a businessman should intelligently invest his capital for long-term profitability? In the grand scheme of economic life first described by Adam Smith, in which nations like individuals should concentrate on the things they do best, how can anyone decide which country produces what most efficiently when the prices change so fast? The answer, to me, must be that such large swings are a symptom of a system in disarray.[17]

Referring to our current hodgepodge of monetary relations as a 'system in disarray' might seem like an understatement. Today's currency disorder is technically no kind of system at all. Although the very reason the IMF was brought into existence was to oversee a fixed exchange rate monetary system anchored by a dollar convertible into gold, today's IMF permits its 187 members to choose any form of exchange arrangement they wish. Nations can allow their currencies to float, or be pegged to another currency or basket of currencies, or they can adopt the currency of another country, or participate in a currency bloc, or form part of a monetary union. Perversely, the IMF imposes only one restriction: member nations are not allowed to peg their currency to gold.[18]

Existing monetary arrangements neither serve the cause of global economic stability nor the interests of free trade. To see US money soar to such heights and sink to such depths, to have the value of the dollar tossed about on a sea of speculative demand, is to bear witness to a currency that has lost its credibility. That the dollar was once the anchor currency for the international monetary system makes the fall from grace all the more grievous.

Recognizing the economic losses imposed by a fluctuating monetary standard hardly acknowledges the moral lapse of a nation that shirked its earlier commitment to providing a trustworthy dollar. But it marks the starting point for finding a better solution.

Part Two

Fixing the Dollar

Is it time to fix the dollar once more, in keeping with the intentions of our Founders? Can beginning principles have application in the modern world of digital finance and electronic money? Is there still an important role for precious metals – gold and silver – to provide monetary discipline and prevent government abuse of legal tender authority?

Looking to the Constitution for key insights into the role of Congress with regard to US money is the most valid approach for considering how best to reform our current monetary system. The dollar is not only the basic unit of account for determining how effectively the interplay of supply and demand can deliver maximum choice and prosperity within the American free-market economy. It is also the most important currency in the world; it serves as the pre-eminent medium of exchange for international trade and financial transactions.

All of which can be deemed a testament to American strength and a legacy of global leadership. But if America is to continue to provide inspiration around the world as a force for good – defending liberty and economic opportunity – we cannot allow the integrity of US money to deteriorate further. At present, our currency is slated to proceed down a path toward intentional debasement, both in terms of domestic purchasing power and as an international monetary unit. This violates the intentions of our Founders, who sought to keep US money removed from government abuse so as to guarantee individual freedom based on rule of law. It also undermines America's commitment to economic opportunity; attempting to seize price 'competitiveness' through dollar debasement means bilking our trade partners. Cheapening the dollar is not competing; it is cheating.

We need to go back to the principles that our Founders instinctively embraced and deliberately enshrined, in both the Constitution and the Coinage Act, to ensure that the money unit for the United States could not be manipulated by those who would subordinate the rule of law to government expediency. We need to restore the dollar's link to an asset of intrinsic worth and immutable value.

In this section, we will assess the current impact of the Federal Reserve and its role in creating an environment which stimulates wrong-headed financial decisions while paralyzing the real economy. Then we will examine an array of proposals to constrain the discretionary authority now exercised by Fed officials. These will range from ideas aimed at narrowing the dual mandate that presently dictates the Fed's mission – achieving maximum employment as well as stable prices – to more sweeping initiatives that would immediately define the dollar in terms of a fixed weight of gold. A more detailed approach will focus on how to achieve the benefits of stabilizing the value of the dollar through a transition process that incorporates the issuance of Treasury bonds redeemable in gold or silver. Finally, an overall agenda for economic growth will be presented. This will highlight sound money in the context of a revitalized American system of limited government and rule of law.

THE ALMIGHTY FED

The Federal Reserve exercises more power and influence over the economy than any other government entity. Its role in banking and finance has vastly expanded since its founding by Congress in 1913. Today, the Fed is charged with:

- ~ conducting the nation's monetary policy. It does this by influencing the monetary and credit conditions in the economy in pursuit of maximum employment, stable prices, and moderate long-term interest rates.

- ~ supervising and regulating banking institutions. In doing so it aims to ensure the safety and soundness of the nation's banking and financial system, and to protect the credit rights of consumers.

- ~ maintaining the stability of the financial system and containing systemic risk that may arise in financial markets.

∼ providing financial services to depository institutions, the US government, and foreign official institutions. This includes playing a major role in operating the nation's payments system.[20]

With such an immense portfolio, perhaps we should not be surprised that the Fed's performance has delivered results that do not satisfy the most fundamental definition of 'sound money'. Money is meant to serve as a meaningful unit of account and a reliable store of value, yet the value of the dollar fluctuates constantly against other major currencies and has lost tremendous value over time in terms of its domestic purchasing power.

According to the research department of the St. Louis branch of the Federal Reserve, the exchange rate between the dollar and the Japanese yen has gone from one dollar being worth 355 yen in August 1971 to one dollar being worth a mere 77 yen in August 2011. This means that the dollar trades for less than one quarter of its former value relative to the yen. Over the same 40-year period, the dollar has also lost more than 70 per cent of its value relative to the euro/German mark.[21]

What's more, for the three major determinants of domestic economic performance noted in the chart below, it's clear that superior results were achieved during the time when the US dollar was convertible into gold under the Bretton Woods system compared to the post-Bretton Woods period from August 1971 to the present.

	(1947-1971)	(1947-2011)
Consumer Price Index	2.5%	4.4%
Real Gross Domestic Product	3.9%	2.8%
Unemployment	4.7%	6.3%

Source: 'The Kudlow Report' on CNBC, August 15, 2011

Inflation has clearly averaged higher in the post-Bretton Woods years as measured by the Consumer Price Index, while real growth has averaged considerably lower. Employment was higher during the Bretton Woods era, further testifying to the economically enhancing properties of a stable monetary environment.

In sum, the Fed has fallen short in providing the same performance on key variables when left to its own discretionary powers unrestrained by the gold convertibility provision of the Bretton Woods system. The Fed has achieved neither maximum employment nor stable prices – its two primary responsibilities – while conducting the nation's monetary policy based on the less-than-omniscient judgment of its Board of Governors.

Decisions to influence the base structure of interest rates are made every five to eight weeks by the Federal Open Market Committee (FOMC), comprising the seven Fed governors (including the Chairman), plus five of the twelve Reserve Bank presidents on a rotating basis. While the decision-making process is aimed at incorporating the recommendations of its members, the Committee must ultimately reach a consensus regarding the appropriate course for policy. Its decision is incorporated in a directive setting forth the Committee's objectives regarding certain key monetary and credit aggregates to the Federal Reserve Bank of New York. This executes day-to-day open-market transactions aimed at easing or constraining the level of reserves available to the banking system.[22]

By influencing the amount of reserves, the Fed attempts to prod banks into making more loans or cutting back. The idea is that the spigot for expanding or contracting the economy can be controlled by monetary policy - in other words, by moving interest rates up or down to alter the lending behavior of banks. Since banks must keep reserves with the Fed, they are sensitive to the price they have to pay to borrow excess reserves from other banks to make additional loans for their own portfolios.

But what happens if nearly all banks have excess reserves – that is, more than they are required to keep with the Fed – because they encounter few opportunities to make viable loans in a weak economy? At what point is the Fed merely 'pushing on a string' when it tries to stimulate banks into making loans through monetary policy that makes funds available at near-zero interest rates? And what should we make of Fed policies that entice banks to make loans not to private sector borrowers, but rather to the US government in the form of Treasury securities?

This serious potential conflict of interest arises because the Federal Reserve is a government agency charged with supervising and regulating banking institutions. At the same time, the Fed provides financial services to the US government and has played a huge role in facilitating bailout programs initiated by the Treasury department. Since early 2011, the Fed has become the largest holder of US Treasury securities, surpassing even China.[21]

Given the inherent conflicts within the Fed's defined responsibilities – in combination with painful deficiencies when it comes to 'maintaining the stability of the financial system and containing systemic risk that may arise in financial markets' – it's no wonder there is growing interest in the subject of monetary reform. People are increasingly discussing how it might be possible to wean a financial system and economy grown reliant on Fed directives to a more market-driven approach to setting interest rates. At what point does 'stimulus' cause more damage to economic prospects than simply allowing prices to find their true level?

Both at home and abroad, the dominance of the Fed in financial markets is being questioned. Now that America's credit rating as a sovereign borrower has been called into question, how much longer can the dollar retain its position as the world's key currency? Is it just a matter of broadening the number of currencies that might be deemed 'reserve' currencies – or have we reached the point where governments, all too prone to spendthrift ways, are in no position to lend credibility to currencies?

MONETARY REFORM: WEIGHING THE OPTIONS

What would it mean to have serious monetary reform? And by 'serious' we mean going beyond mere tinkering with trivial aspects of current decision-making procedures or changing the makeup of the Federal Open Market Committee – including the appointment of a new Fed Chairman. The challenge is rather to bring US money into conformance with American founding principles regarding limited government encroachment on individual freedom.

Is it possible in this modern age to embrace once more the notion embedded in the Constitution that sound money is guaranteed if Congress is empowered to define the value of US money in the same context as establishing official weights and measures for the United States?

If our money was always meant to serve as a standard – from the adoption of the Coinage Act of 1792 through the end of the Bretton Woods international monetary system in August 1971 – how can we return to that guiding principle in both concept and practice?

There is one aspect of US money that can be identified throughout this long monetary history, if not as a constant then nevertheless as a recurrent theme. The dollar was defined in terms of a specific weight of gold or silver, or both. Even though the right to convert into a fixed amount of an asset with intrinsic worth was suspended (during the Civil War) and restricted to foreign governments (under Bretton Woods), it remained the case that the valuation of US money was expressed in terms of precious metals.

Contrast that situation with the implications of this dialog between Congressman Ron Paul and Fed Chairman Ben Bernanke, which took place at a congressional hearing on monetary policy in March 2011:

> Dr. Paul: How can you manage monetary policy, which means to manage the dollar, if we don't have a definition of a dollar? I can't find in the Code what a dollar is or a Federal Reserve note. And everybody knows a Federal Reserve note is a dollar, you create a note, which is a promise to pay, and that is another dollar....I want a definition of money....We want a measurement of value....And you and I will have a disagreement on whether gold is money or not. But the Fed holds gold, the Treasury holds gold, the central bank holds gold....Gold is the true long-term measurement of value. So how can you run your operation without a definition of the dollar, and what is your definition of a dollar?

> Mr. Bernanke: You raise some important points, Congressman. Our mandate is maximum employment and price stability. My definition of the dollar is what it can buy. Consumers don't want to buy gold. They want to buy food and gasoline and clothes and all the other things that are in the consumer basket. It is the buying power of the dollar in terms of those goods and services that is what is important, and that is what I call price stability.[23]

It is hard to reconcile the Fed Chairman's appraisal of what defines a dollar with the constitutional definition; that is, the dollar was clearly meant to serve as a *measure* of value. Indeed, the money unit of the United States might ultimately provide a worldwide standard 'at once invariable and universal', as envisioned by Thomas Jefferson and George Washington. The contrast with this latter-day definition of the dollar based on 'what it can buy' is especially striking given that the Fed's assessment of its mandate to achieve 'price stability' is couched in such oxymoronic terms as 'stable inflation expectations'. And the dismissal of gold in responding to a question about the definition of a dollar seems oddly cavalier for an individual so familiar with US monetary history.

So how can the integrity of the dollar be restored in this modern age of central banking and fiat money? What are the most promising reform proposals for monetary policy?

Discussed here are five approaches: 1) changing the Fed's mandate, 2) adopting a formal rule to guide Fed decision making, 3) incorporating gold price movements into monetary policy, 4) adopting a full gold standard by establishing an official gold convertibility rate for the dollar, and 5) allowing competitive currencies, including private currencies backed by gold or silver, to circulate against Federal Reserve notes. Each will be briefly reviewed with regard to its strengths and weaknesses.

CHANGING THE FED'S MANDATE

The first proposal for monetary reform is aimed at narrowing the broad set of responsibilities currently assigned to the Federal Reserve. It is widely recognized that the so-called 'dual mandate' can sometimes pose a dilemma for members of the Federal Open Market Committee. During times of 'stagflation', which is characterized by both slow economic growth and rising inflation, policymakers have a quandary. Should they ease monetary conditions to stimulate economic activity or rather engage in tightening to prevent further inflation pressures? Should interest rates go up or down?

The dual mandate stems from an economic theory popular in the 1970s that posited a trade-off between inflation and unemployment. It was asserted by 'Phillips Curve' reasoning that aggregate demand could be expanded by increasing the quantity of money. This in turn would result in higher economic growth and employment. Higher prices would result as well, but the goal was to find the optimum trade-off point for maximizing employment while minimizing the price gains.

By 1978, Congress had embraced the notion that such fine-tuning of the economy could be implemented by the Fed through its monetary policy decisions. It adopted the 'Full Employment and Balanced Growth Act' (also known as the Humphrey-Hawkins Full Employment Act), which sought to coordinate monetary policy actions taken by the Chairman of the Federal Reserve with the economic policies of the President.[24] Though the Act expired in 2000, its legacy has remained in the dual mandate of the Fed and the requirement for the Chairman to report to Congress twice annually on monetary policy and the state of the economy.

Those who recognize that the Fed has become an overly dominant force in financial markets are quick to suggest that the responsibility to maximize employment should be eliminated; it leads to excessive government intervention in the economy. Price stability should be the single focus of the nation's central bank, according to Bob Corker, the Republican Senator for Tennessee, a member of the Senate Banking Committee:

> It is time that we work to clarify the mandate of the Federal Reserve. Providing our central bank with a clear and explicit focus on keeping inflation low will serve America better than the broader mandate approach we have today.[25]

However, while it seems helpful to limit the mandate of the Fed so that price stability becomes its chief focus, it is not obvious that actions taken by the FOMC to raise or lower interest rates would significantly vary as a result. True, it would mitigate the inherent policy contradiction that arises from the directive to maximize employment (by expanding the money supply) while keeping inflation low. But as Professor Greg Mankiw of Harvard University has argued, reducing the Fed's dual mandate would not necessarily change its interest rate policy in times of economic weakness. He notes that FOMC members could still make the case for expansionary policy if they felt that deflation, rather than inflation, posed the greater threat to recovery. 'I am skeptical,' Mankiw states. 'If the Fed's mandate were different, monetary policy today might well be the same.'[26]

FORMAL PRICE RULES

Those who would seek to achieve more stable prices as a function of monetary policy are drawn toward rules or mechanisms that would impose restrictions on the discretionary authority of Fed officials. One of the ideas that long has been suggested is to require the Fed to publicly announce the specific inflation rate it expects to attain over a certain time period through its policy actions. 'Inflation targeting' is a strategy aimed at making price stability the primary goal of monetary policy – but herein lies an obvious problem.

If the goal is price stability, why should the methodology for achieving it automatically include an assumption of inflation? While some economists, such as Martin Feldstein, have argued for a zero inflation rate as the long-run goal, it has become acceptable for countries that have embraced inflation targeting to establish target ranges between 1 and 3 per cent. The rationale for deviating from zero is that deflation can lead to financial instability and sharp economic contractions; on the other hand, unwarranted increases in the money supply for the sole purpose of preventing deflation might well lead to financial instability by causing the build-up of asset bubbles.

In any case, when inflation targets are set in terms of acceptable ranges as opposed to explicit rates within a specified time period, the strategy is already compromised. According to Professor Frederic Mishkin of Columbia University, inflation targeting must go beyond merely announcing numerical targets for medium-term inflation. He notes that the central bank must also be held accountable for attaining its inflation objectives.[27] In order to be held accountable, though, a decision must be made with regard to the definition of price stability – and this may not be a straightforward task. 'A specific numerical inflation target would represent an unhelpful and false precision,' noted Alan Greenspan in 2002, while serving as Fed Chairman. 'Rather, price stability is best thought of as an environment in which inflation is so low and stable over time that it does not materially enter into the decisions of households and firms.' In the absence of numerical targets, accountability would seem difficult to achieve.

An alternative to imposing *ex post* sanctions on central bank officials might be to prescribe an *ex ante* rule for guiding monetary policy decisions. Professor John Taylor of Stanford University has developed such a rule to provide recommendations on how the Federal Reserve and other central banks should attempt to set interest rates in response to economic conditions. The formula can be simply expressed by stating: the interest rate should be one-and-a-half times the inflation rate, plus one-half times the gap measuring how much gross domestic product has departed from its normal output level, plus one.[28] Its basic thrust is to reduce arbitrary discretion and add predictability to monetary policy decisions.

Conceived some two decades ago to describe how monetary policy was actually conducted under both Greenspan and Volcker, when inflation was largely suppressed, Taylor emphasizes that the rule is meant to be followed not 'mechanically' but rather should be used as a guideline.[29] Still, the advancement of a rules-based policy over the trend toward increasingly unrestrained discretionary authority and *ad hoc* decision making would seem to be an improvement over current monetary policy.

Gold Price Movements

One way to instill more automatic discipline into monetary policy and ensure a more stable dollar would be to link the universality of gold as a monetary surrogate to the process of determining interest rates. Proposals range from merely bringing considerations of gold price movements into FOMC deliberations to more rigidly structured procedures which would effectively dictate monetary policy actions in direct correspondence with observed changes in the market price of gold.

For example, economist David Malpass recently proposed in the *Wall Street Journal* that the Fed should recognize the connection between high gold prices and widespread concerns about inflation and financial stability. 'Gold at more than $1,800 per ounce is a loud public statement of no confidence in our central bank,' noted Malpass. 'It means people would rather buy gold than hire workers or start businesses – that they don't trust the central bank to maintain the value of their money.'[30] To counter this damaging perception, Malpass suggested that the Fed should provide reassurances to financial markets by championing sound money policies aimed at producing lower gold prices in the future.

Although both Volcker and Greenspan made overt reference to gold prices while at the helm of the Fed – indeed, Greenspan expressed the view in 2004 that central banks were most successful when their actions replicated what would have occurred under a gold standard[31] – there is little evidence that Bernanke takes gold price movements into serious consideration when formulating monetary policy. Asked by the Republican Representative for Wisconsin Paul Ryan, who chairs the House Budget Committee, whether surging gold prices are providing important price signals in terms of the global repercussions from weak currency policies, Bernanke's reply did not acknowledge any direct connection:

> I don't fully understand the movements in the gold price. But I do think there's a great deal of uncertainty and anxiety in financial markets right now, and some people believe that holding gold will be a hedge against the fact that they view many other investments as being risky and hard to predict at this point.[32]

In sharp contrast, businessman Steve Forbes has long contended that the price of gold should be a central factor in determining interest rate policy. 'All the Fed has to do is look at the market price of gold: If it moves outside a certain narrow range, the monetary authorities should react by either tightening or loosening the money supply.'[33] In keeping with the logic that a price rule would rein in discretionary monetary authority, Forbes explains that relinking US money to gold would deliver better results – not only with regard to dollar stability but also in terms of real economic performance. He notes that the Founders, particularly Alexander Hamilton, recognized that a firm dollar was needed to provide a strong and stable foundation for a lawful society. Volatile and ultimately worthless money invariably brings about debilitating consequences and has undermined the economies of whole countries throughout history.[34]

Using a gold price rule to determine whether to expand or contract the issuance of dollars would institute a more formal process for connecting monetary policy to an asset of intrinsic worth. While it might be possible to establish a broad index of goods and services to reflect the general price level, the simplicity and straightforwardness of using the price of gold as a surrogate for changes in the purchasing power of money clearly has advantages. Deviations from the target price of gold, either higher or lower, would elicit remedial action from central bank officials. In short, the money supply would be expanded or contracted as necessary to maintain the steady value of gold in dollars.

GOLD CONVERTIBILITY

What would it take to set up a genuine gold standard with a working mechanism for converting US dollars into gold on demand? The first step would be to address current federal legal tender laws, which require that people must accept paper currency issued by the Federal Reserve as lawful money. Indeed, US currency bills today carry the declaration: 'This note is legal tender for all debts, public and private.' Earlier notes had a somewhat different inscription: 'Redeemable in lawful money at the United States Treasury, or at any Federal Reserve Bank.' Still earlier forms of US paper money, such as the gold certificates issued in the 1920s, stated: 'This certifies that there have been deposited in the Treasury of the United States of America twenty dollars in gold coin payable to the bearer on demand.'

But an individual seeking to convert a Federal Reserve note into lawful money by submitting it to the Treasury or a branch of the Federal Reserve system today would have his paper money returned to him with the tautological explanation: the note itself is, by definition, lawful money. Revoking the government's right to force people to accept its paper notes as legal tender would mark the beginning of the transition toward solid money convertible on demand into a fixed weight of something valuable.

The next major step toward achieving gold convertibility would be to define the US dollar as a fixed weight of gold. Legislation to bring this about would assign to Congress the objective of securing a description of the dollar which accords with a measurable quantity of gold of a certain fineness. This would provide a meaningful unit of account for monetary purposes.

Such a major change from our current practice presents significant challenges in managing the transition. What is the appropriate period of time between an announcement by the US government that it intends to establish, by statute, a weight unit of gold as the dollar monetary standard and the time the actual parity would be officially stipulated? Determining the rate of convertibility would require tracking the value of gold on world markets and estimating the potential impact on price levels, both domestically and abroad, as the United States prepared to go on a gold standard. It is an important calculation. Fixing the dollar price of gold too low could bring on deflation as individuals sought to convert dollars into gold at what seemed a bargain rate, thus contracting the money supply. By contrast, establishing too high a parity between dollars and gold would prompt people to turn in gold for dollars, expanding the money supply and causing inflation.[35]

Still, the advantages of forging an inviolable link between the value of US money and gold through fixed convertibility seem to make it well worth tackling the difficulties. As economist Phillip Cagan, whose work on the monetary dynamics of hyperinflation is considered a classic in the field, has summarized:

> I see no escape from the conclusion, inherent in the position of the advocates of gold, that only a convertible monetary system is sufficiently free of discretion to guarantee that it will achieve price stability. The operation of any inconvertible monetary system introduces a discretion in management that cannot guarantee price stability despite the efficacy of its monetary controls. Of course, no system can guarantee that the system itself will not be tinkered with or abandoned. But if one is looking for some kind of long-lasting commitment of a constitutional nature, a convertible monetary system seems to be the only practical possibility.[36]

Gold convertibility of the dollar would reassert the early principles embedded in both the Constitution and the Coinage Act with regard to establishing a money unit defined as a precise weight of gold or silver. But beyond achieving this congruence with the intentions of the Founders, a dollar relinked to gold would have substantial implications for international currency relations and the global economy. Other major countries would be compelled to evaluate their own policies governing money issuance with an eye toward maintaining the value of individual currencies in the presence of a gold-backed dollar.

Calling for an international monetary conference would reassure the United States' trading partners that their cooperation is welcomed, even solicited. At the same time, given the pre-eminent role of the dollar in global financial markets, it would be seen as an important step toward achieving radical international monetary reform. Lewis Lehrman, an active proponent of the gold standard and former member of President

Ronald Reagan's Gold Commission, testified before Congress in March 2011 that dollar convertibility to gold must not only be restored, it must also become a cooperative project of major nations. 'The world trading community would benefit from such a common currency – a non-national, neutral, monetary standard – that cannot be manipulated and created at will by the government of any one country.' Lehrman recommended that a new Bretton Woods conference should be convened to establish mutual gold convertibility among leading powers.[37]

Not all monetary scholars accept the notion that international conferences play an important role in the transition to fundamentally different monetary regimes. Giulio Gallarotti contends that the success of the classical gold standard from 1880 to 1914 was the result of 'spontaneous order' and not the deliberate efforts of political officials from powerful nations seeking multilateral collaboration on monetary relations:

> The international character of the regime was simply an unintended consequence of the convergence of monetary policies across nations. An orderly and stable system of exchange rates, international interconvertibility, and capital mobility were natural outcomes of nations fixing the price of national currencies to gold, monetary authorities standing ready to buy from and sell gold to anybody, and low restrictions on the importation and exportation of precious metals. Things equal to the same thing are equal to each. And to the extent that nations practiced gold monometallism in a responsible way, which they did, international confidence remained high, as convertibility and exchange risk continued to be perceived to be low. A German monetary official of the period put it best: 'Who needs an international monetary union if everyone is on gold?'[38]

Certainly it is true that the success of a global gold standard depends on each participating nation's commitment to enforcing the fiscal and monetary discipline in their domestic economic policies necessary to maintain the viability of the system on an international basis. Yet while Gallarotti is correct in pointing out that a monetary system such as the classical gold standard can come about only when nations voluntarily agree to abide by the discipline of gold convertibility, he perhaps underestimates the potential usefulness - particularly at a time of widespread economic anxiety - of holding an international monetary conference. There can be no doubt that if the United States put forth a solid proposal to hold such a conference, and at the same time took convincing steps to adopt gold convertibility at home, it would have a profound impact on our top trade partners and the entire global economy.

COMPETING CURRENCIES

Some of the most prominent monetary economists have come to the conclusion that even a gold standard can be compromised by government manipulation. Friedrich Hayek, recipient of the 1974 Nobel Prize in Economics and foremost member of the Austrian school of political economy, would not trust government even to maintain an honest gold standard. But if government cannot be relied on to issue the money, who can? 'I am more convinced than ever that if we ever again are going to have sound money, it will not come from government,' Hayek asserted in November 1977. 'It will be issued by private enterprise.'[39]

But what would it mean to have private enterprise money? It's difficult to think of an asset more public in nature than money. Defining it as the medium of exchange designates its acceptability as a measure of value. Its validity is acknowledged by the parties concerned in any economic transaction. To compete with government-issued money, or to replace it, private money would have to be at least as acceptable to its users as government-issued money. To attain that level of legitimacy would require going beyond legal definitions or economic comparisons; private money would have to be culturally acceptable.

The fact that humans still tend to think of themselves as citizens of specific nation states, subject to the authority of their governments, suggests there might be a higher psychological comfort level associated with using government-issued money. Money has an official air about it with its iconic symbols, numbers and official signatures, its illustrations of cultural heroes and important historical events. It conveys the very essence of national sovereignty. (Indeed, a major design hurdle for the euro was to create reassuring images associated with the traditional monetary authority of individual states while nevertheless avoiding any specific nationalist reference. The solution was to evoke generic landmarks representing historic bridges, arches, and gateways; the images printed on euro banknotes are entirely fictional.)

Just because the issuance of money has long been one of the

sovereign rights claimed by governments, though, does not mean that it cannot be produced and managed more effectively by private enterprise. Indeed, Hayek argued that 'governments have invariably and inevitably grossly abused that power throughout the whole of history' and concluded that a system based on competing private currencies offered a much more promising avenue for achieving sound money.[40] Would private competition to produce money result in a more orderly monetary regime, or would it lead to even greater currency chaos?

People who believe in the efficacy of private money derive their faith from a basic belief in free markets as the least arbitrary, most efficient and fairest mechanism for producing and distributing goods and services for society. Under a laissez-faire monetary regime, competition among money producers would ultimately lead to the development of an identifiable brand of money that would fulfill consumer demands for a reliable unit of account, a store of value and a medium of exchange. To gain more customers, while at the same time retaining old customers, money would have to outperform its competitors. To do that, it would have to become better and better until it provided the ultimate stability in the form of zero inflation for its users. As Richard Rahn, former chief economist at the US Chamber of Commerce, has argued: 'Private issuers of money have stronger incentives than governments to maintain the real purchasing power of a currency because the only way to make a profit by issuing money would be to provide a currency that people consider superior to government money.'[41]

The idea of competing private currencies is theoretically appealing because it embraces free market doctrine to advance the notion that the best money would come about as the result of having to satisfy consumer desires. Given the poor performance of the Federal Reserve and declining public confidence in its abilities to stimulate growth through near-zero interest rates and quantitative easing, it is not surprising that legislation has been introduced to permit private currencies to compete against the dollar. Testifying in favor of House Resolution 1098, a bill known as 'The Free Competition in Currency Act of 2011', economist Lawrence White of George Mason University explains:

> H.R. 1098 would give currency competition a chance. It would not remove the Federal Reserve from the currency market, but it would

give the Fed a stronger incentive to deliver the kind of trustworthy money that consumers want. The dollar already faces salutary international competition from gold, silver, the euro, the Swiss franc, and other stores of value. H.R. 1098 would allow salutary domestic competition between the Federal Reserve Note and other media of exchange. The Fed will have little to fear from competition so long as it provides the highest quality product on the market. Continuing to ban competition from the domestic US currency market, or keeping it at a legal disadvantage, limits the options of American consumers who use money to their disadvantage.[42]

Even so, there remains a fundamental question of whether consumers want to have a choice when it comes to money. History has shown that people have a remarkable loyalty to money that offers familiarity, even long after that currency has been debased by government and even when alternatives are available. Some of this reluctance to move to unfamiliar currencies is not irrational; there are information costs associated with accepting a new medium of exchange. There is always the risk, too, that the next person may not be willing to accept the new currency – a possibility that detracts from the seeming superiority of an alternative form of money.

One of the important features of money is the sense of confidence it imparts as a measure for evaluating other goods and services. A monetary regime of competing private currencies potentially adds another layer of complexity to the process an individual experiences when making economic and financial decisions. To the extent there are negative aspects in having to choose among currencies, a dominant producer would likely arise as consumers rallied around the most familiar form of money. Indeed, the more popular a certain brand of currency became, the more it would capture the market; eventually it could become the only readily accepted form of money as people voluntarily chose to use it. The supposed advantages of private competitive currencies would then disappear as the most successful money producer attained a de facto monopoly.

But if the ultimate outcome of a private market for money is a monopoly, does it make much difference whether the monopoly is run by a private company versus a public entity? While the former case could lead to economic exploitation based on a market advantage, the threat of potential competition would inhibit this tendency. The latter case, however, invites a more sinister abuse of government power – even tyranny – as government precludes market entry to alternative issuers.

As long as people are confident that the currency is redeemable into real assets on demand, they may be indifferent. By habit and by history, though, it would seem that citizens are largely predisposed to grant government the power to issue money. The question is how to ensure that the integrity of money is upheld.

TREASURY TRUST BONDS

President Reagan famously distilled his wise approach on arms relations with the former Soviet Union into the phrase: 'Trust, but verify'. It captured the idea that both parties were dealing honorably and could be trusted to uphold agreements – but also granted the right to ensure that the original terms were fulfilled.

Such an approach hearkens back to the nature of the monetary contract expressed on a special class of gold certificates issued in 1922 on which it is stated: 'This certifies that there have been deposited in the Treasury of the United States of America twenty dollars in gold coin payable to the bearer on demand.' These gold certificates were known as 'horse blankets' because they were somewhat larger than other paper currency issued by the US government.[43] They carried a portrait of George Washington and could be exchanged for the equivalent amount in gold coin at the option of the holder. The Treasury also issued silver certificates that were likewise backed by physical holdings of silver retained in government vaults.

The fundamental dissonance in the implicit monetary contract that exists today between the US government and those of us who hold dollars is this: We have no way to verify that the value of our money will be upheld. There is no government-certified mechanism by which dollars can be redeemed in an asset of recognized worth at a fixed price by mutual consent. So if we make contracts to buy or sell goods, to loan money or seek funds from investors – and the agreement is denominated in dollars – we have already raised the distinct possibility that the terms of the agreement may be significantly altered by factors seemingly beyond our control. In other words, those dollars may be worth considerably less in the future than their current value. How can the contractual obligations of any financial agreement be meaningfully enforced if the monetary unit of account is subject to unpredictable changes in its value?

When the Chairman of the Federal Reserve defines the dollar in terms of 'what it can buy' at any given moment rather than invoking the doctrine of America's earlier monetary authorities, such as Roger Sherman, who inveighed against the negative consequences of a fluctuating medium of exchange, it's evident that we need to get back to founding principles. Money is a moral contract between the government and those who hold its currency, as described by Domingo Cavallo, the former finance minister of Argentina who succeeded in halting rampant inflation in his country by ensuring that every peso issued by the government was backed by a dollar or gold in reserves. Noting that you could substitute dollar or any other currency in describing that moral contract, American financier Ted Forstmann elaborated:

> That contract guarantees that each peso – as a unit of value that the holder has worked hard to get – will be worth as much tomorrow as today. If the government breaks the contract, it's breaking the law. The only role of government in the economy should be to guarantee the integrity of market transactions.[44]

The guarantee of integrity must begin with the currency itself – it must begin with sound money. Would our government be willing to redeem a special class of Treasury obligations in *either* dollars or gold at maturity? Would it stand ready to honor an agreement to repay holders of a debt instrument – denoted as 'Treasury Trust Bonds' – the promised amount of principal at maturity as expressed as a nominal dollar amount *or* a specific weight of gold?

Potential interest in such an instrument would reflect the concerns of those who accept that Treasury bonds are debt obligations issued and backed by the full faith and credit of the US government. While lenders may believe that the borrower will perform honorably in repaying the amount borrowed, having the option to be paid in gold by mutual agreement beforehand provides a solid guarantee of value.

In the following section, further details are provided on how this trust-yet-verify provision of a Treasury security might be structured.

A Dollar As Good As Gold

Restoring the integrity of US money can begin with a limited issuance of Treasury obligations denominated in terms of a dollar that is literally 'as good as gold'. Treasury Trust Bonds would incorporate familiar investment securities and the concept is straightforward. Imagine you have the opportunity today to purchase a debt instrument from the Treasury with a principal amount of $2,400 and a five-year maturity date; at the end of five years, you will have the option to receive either $2,400 or one troy ounce of gold. How much would you be willing to pay for that instrument?

Investors who think the dollar price of gold will be considerably higher than that amount five years from now – because they suspect too many dollars will be printed in the meantime – will likely pay a substantial premium for Treasury Trust Bonds redeemable in gold. They would effectively be purchasing a US government obligation priced similarly to a conventional Treasury bill, on which the rate of interest is inherent in the difference between the purchase price and the face amount received at maturity.[45] But they would also be purchasing a call option on gold, so if the dollar price for a troy ounce of gold in five years' time is higher than $2,400, they could instead choose to exercise the option of receiving payment in the form of physical gold (one troy ounce) or its dollar equivalent at time of redemption, in accordance with bondholder instructions.

For potential purchasers of Treasury Trust Bonds, it would be comparable to buying a variation of Treasury Inflation-Protected Securities (TIPS), which the US government has made available to investors since January 1997. The incentive for offering an inflation-linked bond was to provide investors with the ability to protect against inflation while providing a certain real return over the investment period. A normal or 'nominal' bond pays its interest on a fixed principal amount, which is repaid at maturity. Inflation is a major risk to a nominal bondholder, since increasing inflation means reduced purchasing power in the face of increasing prices.

With the creation of TIPS, those willing to lend money to the US government were able to ensure – for the first time – that no loss of purchasing power in dollar terms would diminish the value of the investment over the time to maturity. In the same way, the introduction of Treasury Trust Bonds would protect investors in US government debt against loss of purchasing power in terms of gold. Whereas TIPS reimburse the bondholder for the impact of inflation as measured by the Consumer Price Index (CPI), Treasury Trust Bonds would reimburse the bondholder for the impact of inflation as measured by the dollar price of gold.

Here it is important to clarify that the term 'inflation' as commonly used only measures changes in the price level of consumer goods and services typically purchased by households. Yet the most damaging aspect of excessive issuance of money is arguably manifested in ominous asset bubbles – which can suddenly burst – rather than perpetual low-grade inflation over a long period of time. While chronic inflation at seemingly benign rates does eventually distort price signals, leading to misallocations of capital, the sort of financial panics that prove most debilitating to whole economies are usually the result of some unanticipated meltdown in financial markets related to a specific type of credit instrument or derivative. To the extent that gold is a surrogate for an array of commodities traded worldwide, changes in the dollar price of gold can provide early warning that overly expansionary US monetary policy is fueling asset bubbles.

The objective of offering gold-backed Treasury Trust Bonds - silver-backed bonds which would be similarly structured - is to establish a commitment by the US government to preserve the integrity of the dollar as a meaningful standard of value. It would be an important marker on the road to sound money, a concrete act toward restoring the Constitution's guarantee of stable money through dollar issuance constrained by convertibility into gold or silver.

MAKING IT WORK

The need to reassert economic confidence through monetary stability, both domestically and internationally, should compel US policymakers to launch Treasury Trust Bonds as a meaningful initiative for dollar reform.

Considerations for issuing the first series of gold-backed U.S. debt obligations should include:

∼ Whether initially to restrict the purchase of these instruments in the same way Series EE Savings Bonds are currently restricted. These are subject to a maximum purchase of $5,000 per calendar year per entity. In addition, to own US Savings Bonds you must be a US resident or US citizen living abroad (with a US address of record) and have been issued with a Social Security Number.

~ Treasury Trust Bonds could be enacted either through legislation or as an initiative by the Treasury department in consultation with the Federal Reserve. Legislation would specifically authorize the issuance of five-year Treasury securities that pay no interest but provide for payment of principal at maturity in either ounces of gold or the face value of the security, at the option of the holder. The instrument is an obligation of the US government to redeem the nominal value ('face value') in terms of a precise weight of gold stipulated in advance or the dollar amount established as the monetary equivalent. The rate of convertibility is permanent throughout the life of the bond; it defines the gold value of the dollar.

~ A portion of US official gold holdings presently carried as Treasury assets and pledged to the Federal Reserve as 'Gold certificates' on its balance sheet should be set aside as collateral to provide adequate cover for outstanding redemption obligations engendered by the issuance of Treasury Trust Bonds. If an initial offering encumbered 12 million ounces of gold that could potentially be called, it would represent less than 4.6 per cent of US official gold reserves of 261.5 million ounces (8,133.5 tonnes). Subsequent offerings over the next three years, each maturing in five years, could likewise allocate 12 million ounces of gold each time for a total commitment of 48 million ounces for Treasury Trust Bonds issued annually as part of a four-year test program. The total exposure of potential gold redemption would equal 18.4 per cent of US government holdings; both the Treasury and the Fed carry these official gold reserves at a value of $42.22 versus current market value.[46]

~ Auction bidding for initial and subsequent annual issuances of gold-backed Treasury Trust Bonds would reveal the level of public confidence in fiat dollar obligations versus gold. Yield spreads would clearly reflect aggregate expectations of their comparative medium-term values. If market expectations anticipate dollar inflation - in other words, a decline in the future purchasing power of the dollar - the bonds would sell at a premium over their face value. If inflationary concerns have been stemmed by fiscal adjustments to reduce budget deficits, thus mitigating fears of monetary accommodation through expansionary policies, holders of Treasury Trust Bonds would have little incentive to redeem in gold. The bonds would sell at close to par value if the dollar were expected to remain stable against the value of gold.

∿ The Federal Reserve should utilize the information properties inherent in the yields of Treasury Trust Bonds to evaluate investor expectations. It would measure the comparative yields on gold-backed US government obligations with conventional Treasury bonds of the same maturity. Just as inflation-indexed bonds (TIPS) provide an indication of inflation expectations as measured by the CPI, gold-backed Treasury Trust Bonds would provide Fed policymakers with useful feedback regarding aggregate estimates of the dollar's future value as measured by a widely-recognized monetary surrogate for purchasing power.

In summary, Treasury Trust Bonds would provide security to investors who are willing to hold US debt obligations but do not wish to have the value of their investment reduced through debasement of the monetary unit of account in which its contractual terms are denominated. An instrument that embodies a commitment to maintain the value of the dollar in terms of constant purchasing power will function as a barometer on the credibility of the Fed's eventual exit strategy from its lengthy and large-scale quantitative easing operations. US debtholders may well require new assurances – in the form of Treasury Trust Bonds – that fiscal irresponsibility will not be redressed through inflationary monetary policies.

AGENDA: GETTING TO GOLD

For those who sense that the restoration of American values must start by reasserting beginning principles, including the commitment to a reliable monetary standard, it is clear that the dollar must be fixed. It is a broken currency. No longer does the dollar function as a vital measuring tool for individuals engaged in voluntary free market transactions; its value is determined by government decisions to expand or contract the supply of dollars. Its meaning as a monetary standard has no relation to intrinsic worth but is rather a credit note issued by government that has been declared legal tender.

This is exactly what the Founders sought to disallow. In defining the money unit of the United States, it was recognized from the beginning that an unstable, unreliable money unit would lead to the dissolution of a new nation – and along with it, all the dreams of individual liberty and economic opportunity that a self-governing people aspired to achieve. Thomas Jefferson believed that America's new money should provide a common currency that was trustworthy. This meant that every citizen could understand what a dollar represented in terms of its purchasing power, in terms of a precise weight of gold or silver. For Jefferson, a dollar was never to be an abstract, fluctuating notion of value favored by economists and specialists, clouded by complex calculations, and susceptible to manipulation and speculation. It was to be based on the principles of simplicity, rationality, familiarity and integrity.

How can we recapture the commitment to honest money – to knowing what a dollar stands for, what it represents as a unit of account and a store of value – without reasserting the wisdom of the Founders in limiting the power of government through deliberately-structured constraints? The link to precious metals so vital in defining the dollar not only provided the cornerstone for developing an American economy based on free market capitalism, it was also the stabilizing and coherent key to economic integration with the rest of the world. By defining the dollar in gold and silver, America was prepared to engage with trade partners across the seas as readily as across the borders of newly-united states. Money is the language of commerce; it communicates the message of supply and demand through price signals. The clarity of those price signals is a function of the precision of the medium of exchange. To have a common currency is to embrace a common belief that free markets provide the best opportunity for individuals to pursue their highest economic aspirations – and for whole societies to achieve maximum prosperity.

Today the challenge of defining the dollar both in order to establish the necessary foundation for real economic growth domestically and to facilitate meaningful global monetary reform requires getting to gold.

To the unsophisticated, it may seem a throwback; after all, the world was on a gold standard in the last century. What lessons are applicable in our modern age? Just as Americans are rediscovering the principled monetary insights of those who framed the Constitution, the restoration of gold as a universally-acknowledged store of value is also drawing the attention of those with a global perspective. Robert Zoellick, a former Treasury official who now presides over the World Bank, has suggested a potential role for gold in a new international monetary system dedicated to economic growth and free trade. 'The system should also consider employing gold as an international reference point of market expectations about inflation, deflation and future currency values,' Zoellick stated. 'Although textbooks may view gold as the old money, markets are using gold as an alternative monetary asset today.'[47]

The benefit of offering Treasury Trust Bonds as an interim approach to a new gold standard is that linking the dollar to gold becomes the objective – whether this is ultimately achievable as the result of a deliberate government policy or as a consequence of allowing private competitive currency options to exist in parallel. If demand for Treasury Trust Bonds exceeds the limited issuance authorized by legislation or enacted under the directive of a Treasury secretary, one would expect private market firms to replicate the same financial instrument. They would combine gold futures contracts with conventional Treasury bonds, effectively providing the same investment vehicle with the same provisions for payment at maturity. While the active participation of the US government in designing and administering a program for issuing Treasury Trust Bonds establishes the intent of the United States officially to make the dollar as good as gold, it does not preclude the involvement of private financial firms toward that end. Indeed, by harnessing the vast investment resources of financial firms in the private sector, the transition toward a new gold standard will be accomplished with greater market depth and rapidity.

Moreover, investment demand for Treasury Trust Bonds would provide a signal to other nations that the United States had established a beachhead for building a gold-based monetary system. China would in all probability be the first country to emulate such an offering with its own gold-convertible bonds. The yuan closely tracks the dollar in foreign exchange markets, so China incurs little risk by following the US lead in issuing a sovereign debt instrument featuring the gold option clause. China is likely to welcome the opportunity to reinforce the US commitment to fiscal discipline inherent in gold-convertible Treasury Trust Bonds. And other countries with large holdings of gold reserves – Germany, Italy, France and Japan – might well decide to demonstrate their own allegiance to monetary stability through the issuance of gold-backed bonds. Pooling gold collateral among eurozone nations wishing to participate in euro-denominated bond offerings could ultimately lead to the joint issuance of gold-linked financial instruments. With successively larger issuances among a broader group of countries, a convergence toward monetary stability centered on gold will lead to fixed exchange rates – and effectively, a common currency based on a universal monetary unit of account defined as a precise weight of gold.

SOUND AND STABLE MONEY

One thing to keep in mind when pursuing the cause of sound money is this: Money is a tool, not an end in itself. It enables individuals to evaluate economic and financial choices, to conduct voluntary transactions with each other, to save and invest for future generations. In short, money allows us to establish priorities and meet obligations day by day, as well as to make plans for the future.

If the money is broken, our capacity to pursue the opportunities available to us in a free society is grossly impaired. Our ability to explore options and make responsible decisions is distorted by misleading price signals and ambiguous messages about what can be expected in our financial future. People have demanded sound money throughout history because they sense that the assertion of sovereign authority over money issuance often ends up benefiting the sovereign more than the people.

Renewed interest in restoring the integrity of the dollar is in keeping with a broader movement to renew America's dedication to free enterprise and limited government. It reflects a belief in the promise of traditional American solutions to problems: Unleash the creative energies of individuals, reassert the primacy of the private sector and remove the heavy yoke of convoluted taxation, burdensome regulation and unpredictable economic outlook from around the necks of would-be entrepreneurs. Confidence begins with sound money and the certainty of knowing that a dollar today will be worth a dollar tomorrow.

'What makes our Constitution such an extraordinary document is that, in making the United States the freest civilization in history, the Founders guaranteed that it would become the most prosperous as well,' noted Paul Ryan in a recent address to Hillsdale College. 'The American system of limited government, low taxes, sound money and the rule of law has done more to help the poor than any other economic system ever designed.'[48] Restoring that guarantee must be part of any US agenda for economic renewal and regeneration.

In honoring the wisdom and perpetuating the insights of our Founders, we need to resurrect the original commitment of Jefferson and Washington, as well as Madison, Hamilton and Sherman, to a dollar defined by its intrinsic worth – not as a shackle but rather an anchor. As recently as the Reagan era, not long ago when traced against the arc of American monetary history across two centuries, Jack Kemp offered this assessment before an assemblage that included Fed Chairman Paul Volcker, the governors of the Federal Reserve Board, and the chairmen of the regional Federal Reserve banks:

> It is no secret that I strongly believe that the dollar must again be defined and convertible into gold, in order to restore long-term credibility in the bond and mortgage markets. A gold guarantee hedges dollar assets and liabilities against sustained inflation or the default risk of deflation. It provides the world with an anchor, a reasonably predictable unit of account for making contracts across borders and between generations. A gold standard provides the issuers of currency with a prompt error signal for adjusting policy – something we sorely need.[49]

It was shortly after the Reagan administration came into power at the beginning of the 1980s that the question of restoring the gold standard was taken up by a commission of 17 individuals appointed by President Reagan. Among them were such staunch advocates as Ron Paul and Lewis Lehrman, who continue to make a persuasive case today that the discipline of gold convertibility is vital to restoring the integrity of the dollar. In September 1981, Alan Greenspan made the observation in a *Wall Street Journal* op-ed article that 'growing disillusionment with politically controlled monetary policies has produced an increasing number of advocates for a return to the gold standard – including at times

President Reagan.' Expanding on the widening interest in bold proposals for monetary reform, Greenspan noted:

> In years past a desire to return to a monetary system based on gold was perceived as nostalgia for an era when times were simpler, problems less complex and the world not threatened with nuclear annihilation. But after a decade of destabilizing inflation and economic stagnation, the restoration of a gold standard has become an issue that is clearly rising on the economic policy agenda.[50]

Greenspan went so far as to suggest that the feasibility of returning to a gold standard might be tested through the issuance of five-year Treasury notes payable in gold. 'The degree of success of restoring long-term fiscal confidence will show up clearly in the yield spreads between gold and fiat dollar obligations of the same maturities,' he explained. 'Full convertibility would require that the yield spread for all maturities virtually disappear.'[51]

Though it would be six years before Greenspan would be appointed Chairman of the Federal Reserve, he clearly recognized that meaningful link between the restoration of fiscal confidence and the discipline imposed by gold convertibility of the dollar. It's interesting to speculate how economic and financial developments might have turned out differently had the US adopted such a proposal at the time.

Still, when an idea has merit – and holds out the potential to help restore the principles and values that can underpin economic renewal – it is never too late. Endeavoring to probe whether it might be useful to offer Treasury bonds payable in gold today, with the same objective of ascertaining the feasibility of returning to a gold standard, Senator Jim DeMint asked Fed Chairman Ben Bernanke: 'Have you given any thought to the idea of issuing bonds payable in gold that would begin to create some standard for our currency?' Bernanke acknowledged that a gold standard 'did deliver price stability over very long periods of time' while insisting it was not a 'panacea' for today's economic ills.[52]

The proposal for Treasury Trust Bonds presented here clearly finds its antecedents in Greenspan's 1981 recommendation but it goes back much farther, proclaiming its most profound legacy in the commitment of the early architects of America to an unchanging monetary standard. To establish a money unit for the United States worthy of universal recognition was to abide by unwavering principles consistent with America's vision for self-government based on equal rights and rule of law.

A trustworthy dollar was testimony to the honest ambitions and remarkable capabilities of a striving people dedicated to freedom. It paid tribute to their unprecedented success, inspiring even greater performance in the future.

It can still do so.

We must fix the dollar now.

ENDNOTES

PART ONE

1. Thomas Jefferson, 'Notes on the Establishment of a Money Unit, and of a Coinage for the United States,' April, 1784, from *The Works of Thomas Jefferson,* Federal Edition (New York and London: G. P. Putnam's Sons, 1904-5), Vol.4.

2. Roger Sherman, 'A Caveat Against Injustice, or an Inquiry into the Evil Consequences of a Fluctuating Medium of Exchange,' (1752). Available at www.rogershermansociety.org/caveat.htm.

3. Ibid.

4. *The writings of George Washington: being his correspondence, addresses, messages, and other papers, official and private*, Volume 9 (Google eBook), p. 186.

5. Ibid., p. 232.

6. http://press-pubs.uchicago.edu/founders/print_documents/a1_10_1s2.html.

7. *History of the United States of America: from the discovery of the ...,* Volume 6. By George Bancroft (Google eBook), p. 301.

8. Washington, First Annual Message to Congress, Jan. 8, 1790. Available at www.pbs.org/georgewashington/collection/other_1790jan8.html.

9. Washington, Oct. 25, 1791. The patriot's monitor: or, Speeches and addresses of the late George Washington (Google eBook), p. 56.

10. Section 19, 'The Coinage Act of April 2, 1792,' (a Stat. 246). http://nesara.org/files/coinage_act_1792.pdf.

11. Ibid., Section 11.

12. Ibid., Section 14.

13. J. M. McPherson, *Battle cry of freedom: the Civil War era.* (New York, NY: Oxford University Press, 1988), pp. 445 and 446.

14. One troy ounce contains 480 grains, so one ounce of gold was worth 480 divided by 23.22, which equals $20.671835.

15. H. D. White, 'Preliminary Draft Proposal for a United Nations Stabilization Fund and a Bank for Reconstruction and Development of the United and Associated Nations,' draft dated April 1942. In J. K. Horsefield (ed.) *The International Monetary Fund, 1945-65,* vol. III: *Documents,* p. 46.

16. US Department Of Labor, Bureau of Labor Statistics, Washington DC 20212, Consumer Price Index. (See http://www.bls.gov/data/inflation_calculator.htm).

17. Paul Volcker and Toyoo Gyohten, *Changing Fortunes: The World's Money and the Threat to American Leadership* (New York: Times Books, 1992), p. 246.

18. International Monetary Fund, 'About the IMF: End of Bretton Woods System.' (See web site www.imf.org/external/about/histend.htm).

PART TWO

19. *The Federal Reserve System: Purposes & Functions* (Washington DC: Board of Governors of the Federal Reserve System, Ninth Edition, June 2005), p. 1.

20. Federal Reserve Bank of St. Louis: Economic Research/Exchange Rates/Monthly Rates. (See http://research.stlouisfed.org/fred2/categories/95)

21. The Federal Reserve Board: The Structure of the Federal Reserve System/The Federal Open Market Committee (See http://www.federalreserve.gov/pubs/frseries/frseri2.htm)

22. Michael Mackenzie, 'Fed passes China in Treasury holdings,' *Financial Times,* Feb. 2, 2011.

23. 'Monetary Policy and the State of the Economy,'Hearing Before the Committee on Financial Services, US House of Representatives, March 2, 2011 (Washington: US Government Printing Office, 2011), p.14. (See http://financialservices.house.gov/uploadedfiles/112-11.pdf) .

24. Full title: An Act to translate into practical reality the right of all Americans who are able, willing, and seeking to work the full opportunity for useful paid employment at fair rates of compensation; to assert the responsibility of the Federal Government to use all practicable programs and policies to promote full employment, production, and real income, balanced growth, adequate productivity growth, proper attention to national priorities, and reasonable price stability; to require the President each year to set further explicit short-term and medium-term economic goals; to achieve a better integration of general and structural economic policies; and to improve the coordination of economic policymaking within the Federal Government.

25. Coker Urges Change to Fed's Dual Mandate,' Nov. 16, 2010. See website: http://corker.senate.gov.

26. Annalyn Censky, 'Republicans to Fed: Forget about Jobs,' Dec. 3, 2010, CNNMoney.com.

27. Frederic S. Mishkin, 'Inflation Targeting,' in Howard Vane and Brian Snowdon, *Encyclopedia of Macroeconomics* (Edward Elgar: Cheltenham U.K., 2002): 361-65.

28. John Taylor, 'Taylor Rule Change Will Hurt Fed's Inflation Fight,' Bloomberg, Aug. 24, 2009.

29. Ibid.

30. David Malpass, 'Beyond the Gold and Bond Bubbles,' *The Wall Street Journal,* Aug. 31, 2011.

31. Hearing before the Committee on Financial Services, US House of Representatives, July 21, 2004.

32. Hearing before the Committee on the Budget, US House of Representatives, June 9, 2010.

33. Steve Forbes, 'Hamilton Got It Right – Why Can't We?' Jan. 28, 2009 on Forbes.com.

34. Ibid.

35. Judy Shelton, *Money Meltdown: Restoring Order to the Global Currency System* (New York: Free Press, 1994), pp. 302-3.

36. Phillip Cagan, 'A Compensated Dollar: Better or More Likely Than Gold?' in *The Search for Stable Money,* edited by James A. Dorn and Anna J. Schwartz (Chicago and London: University of Chicago Press, 1987), pp. 268-69.

37. Statement and Testimony of Lewis E. Lehrman, Hearing before the Subcommittee on Domestic Monetary Policy and Technology of the Committee on Financial Services, US House of Representatives, March 17, 2011.

38. Giulio M. Gallarotti, 'The Classical Gold Standard as a Spontaneous Order (Centralized Versus Decentralized International Monetary Systems: The Lessons of the Classical Gold Standard),' preliminary draft of paper prepared for the Cato Institute Seventh Annual Monetary Conference, Washington DC., Feb. 23-24, 1989, p. 5. In the last line, the author is paraphrasing a statement appearing in Stanley Zucker, *Ludwig Bamberger: German Liberal Politician and Social Critic* (Pittsburgh: University of Pittsburgh Press, 1975).

39. F. A. Hayek, 'Toward a Free-Market Monetary System,' reprinted in *Search for Stable Money,* ed. Dorn and Schwartz, p. 383.

40. F. A. Hayek, 'Denationalisation of Money - The Argument Refined,' Hobart paper 70, 2nd (extended) ed. (London: Institute of Economic Affairs, 1978), pp.116-17. Quoted in James A. Dorn, ed. *The Cato Journal,* vol. 9, no. 2, Fall 1989, p. 277.

41. Richard W. Rahn, 'Private Money: An Idea Whose Time Has Come,' *The Cato Journal,* vol. 9, no. 2,Fall 1989, pp. 355-56.

42. Lawrence H. White, 'Statement on HR 1098: The Free Competition in Currency Act of 2011,' before the Subcommittee on Domestic Monetary Policy and Technology of the Committee on Financial Services, US House of Representatives, Sept. 13, 2011.

43. Gold certificates measure 7.25 inches long by 3 inches wide as compared with other US banknotes measuring 6.14 inches long by 2.61 inches wide.

44. Theodore J. Forstmann, 'The Paradox of the Statist Businessman,' *Cato Policy Report,* March/April 1995.

45. Treasury bills are short-term government securities with maturities ranging from a few days to 52 weeks. Bills are sold at a discount from their face value.

46. The official price of gold in dollars was raised from $38.02 in December 1971 to $42.22 in February 1973. The US government holds 261,498,899.316 fine troy ounces of gold for a total book value of $11,041,058,821.09 based on book value per troy ounce calculated at $42.2222 official price. See 'Status Report of US Treasury-Owned Gold,' Financial Management Service, Department of the Treasury, Aug. 31, 2011.

47. Robert Zoellick, 'The G20 must look beyond Bretton Woods II,' *Financial Times,* Nov. 7, 2010.

48. 'Restoring the Rule of Law,' Congressman Ryan address to Hillsdale College, Sept. 15, 2011. See http://paulryan.house.gov/News/DocumentSingle.aspx?DocumentID=261843.

49. Jack Kemp, 'An Economic Policy for Economic Recovery,' Remarks before the Board of Governors and Chairmen of the Federal Reserve System, Washington DC, June 2, 1983. Published in *The American Idea: Ending Limits to Growth* (Washington DC: The American Studies Center, 1984), pp. 91-92.

50. Alan Greenspan, 'Can the US Return to a Gold Standard?' *The Wall Street Journal,* Sept. 1, 1981.

51. Ibid.

52. 'The Semiannual Monetary Report to Congress' before the United States Senate Committee on Banking, Housing & Urban Affairs, Washington DC, March 1, 2011.

About the Author

Judy Shelton is an economist with expertise in global finance and monetary issues. She is co-director of the Sound Money Project at the Atlas Economic Research Foundation. Author of *The Coming Soviet Crash* (1989), *Money Meltdown* (1994), and *A Guide to Sound Money* (2010), her international economics articles have been published by *The Wall Street Journal, New York Times, Washington Post, Financial Times, Nihon Keizai Shimbun* and *El Economista*. She has given expert testimony before the Joint Economic Committee, Senate Banking, Senate Foreign Relations, House Banking, and House Foreign Affairs committees. She was a research fellow at the Hoover Institution at Stanford University (1985-1995) and visiting professor of international finance at DUXX Graduate School of Business in Monterrey, Mexico (1995-2001). She was a staff economist for the National Commission on Economic Growth and Tax Reform chaired by Jack Kemp (1995-1996) and has served on the boards of Hilton Hotels and Atlantic Coast Airlines. She is a member of the Joint Advisory Board of Economists for the Commonwealth of Virginia. In January 2010 she became Vice Chairman of the Board of Directors of the National Endowment for Democracy; she is the Board's regional expert on Russia, Ukraine and Belarus and also serves on the Budget and Audit Committee. Dr. Shelton holds a Ph.D. in business administration from the University of Utah.

ABOUT ATLAS ECONOMIC RESEARCH FOUNDATION

Since 1981, Atlas has helped develop independent think tanks, in the U.S. and around the world, that can move public policy debate in the direction of greater liberty. The Atlas network now involves more than 400 think tanks in 80+ countries. Atlas programs and services connect these organizations to the tools, training, and resources they need to succeed.

Atlas does not accept government funding, and depends entirely on voluntary contributions. To learn more about Atlas, visit *AtlasNetwork.org*.

ABOUT THE SOUND MONEY PROJECT

Launched in January 2009, the Sound Money Project at the Atlas Economic Research Foundation is engaging experts in the task of developing and refining a set of "sound money" principles with relevance to the world's current challenges. The project mobilizes think tanks and scholars, including Atlas's resident Sound Money Fellows, to be more active in promoting public policies that are consistent with these principles.

To get more involved, visit our website **SoundMoneyProject.org** or our Facebook page, Sound Money.

To support this effort, you can donate online at *AtlasNetwork.org/Donate* or send your tax-deductible gift to:

> Atlas Economic Research Foundation
> c/o Sound Money Project
> 1201 L Street NW, Second Floor
> Washington, DC 20005